Animal Lives

TIGERS

Sally Morgan

QEB Publishing

QEB

Copyright © QEB Publishing, Inc. 2004

Published in the United States by
QEB Publishing, Inc
23062 La Cadena Drive
Laguna Hills, CA 92653

This edition specially created for
Books Are Fun 2006

Library of Congress Control Number:
2004101324

ISBN 978-1-59566-312-2

Written by Sally Morgan
Designed by Q2A Solutions
Editor Christine Harvey
Map by PCGraphics (UK) Ltd

Creative Director Louise Morley
Editorial Manager Jean Coppendale

Printed and bound in China

The words in **bold** are
explained in the Glossary
on page 31.

Contents

The tiger

The tiger is the largest cat in the world. It is easy to recognize, with its coat of red-orange and dark stripes. The tiger is a powerful hunter. It has sharp teeth, strong jaws, and a muscular body. The tiger is a carnivore; this means that it eats other animals.

The tiger is a fierce hunter and its diet consists entirely of meat.

Endangered animal

The tiger is an **endangered** animal. There are only between 5,000 and 7,000 tigers surviving in the wild.

Tiger

The largest known Siberian tiger weighed 1,027 pounds.

fact

Mammals

The tiger belongs to a group of animals called **mammals**. Other mammals include lions, horses, and humans.

Unlike some big cats, tigers like to live alone.

Types of tigers

Very few white Bengal tigers live in the wild. Most are found in zoos.

There is only one species, or type, of tiger. This species is divided into five subspecies. These are the Sumatran, Siberian or Amur, Bengal or Indian, South China, and Indo-Chinese tigers.

Tiger

White Bengal tigers are rare. Most of them have blue eyes!

fact

The Siberian tiger is the largest of all the tigers and has a long, thick coat.

The best-known tiger is the Bengal tiger of India. The rarest tiger is the small South China tiger—there are only about 30 of them. The smallest tiger is the Sumatran tiger.

Once there were three other subspecies of tiger—the Bali, Java, and Caspian tigers. Sadly, all these tigers are now **extinct**.

Tiger numbers around the world	
Bengal	3,100—4,500
Siberian	360—400
Indo-Chinese	1,200—1,800
Sumatran	400—500
South China	20—30

7

Where do you find tigers?

Bengal tigers often charge into water to catch samba deer that live nearby.

One hundred years ago, tigers were found across the continent of Asia. Now they are found in far fewer places. Some tigers live in countries where it gets very cold, for example in parts of North Korea, eastern Russia, and China. Other tigers live where the climate is warmer, such as India and parts of South-East Asia.

The Siberian tiger has the thickest fur of all the tiger species to keep it warm in the cold Siberian winters.

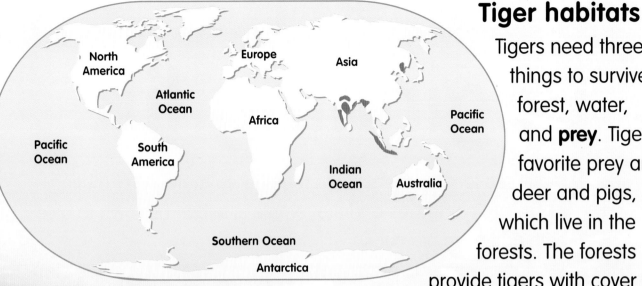

North America

Europe

Asia

Atlantic Ocean

Africa

Pacific Ocean

Pacific Ocean

South America

Indian Ocean

Australia

Southern Ocean

Antarctica

■ Areas where tigers are found.

Tiger habitats

Tigers need three things to survive: forest, water, and **prey**. Tigers' favorite prey are deer and pigs, which live in the forests. The forests provide tigers with cover when they hunt, as well as places where they can hide.

Tigers live in different types of forest, including tropical rainforests, conifer forests, and mixed oak forests.

Tiger

No two tigers have the same pattern of stripes.

fact

9

Beginning life

Male and female tigers come together to mate. After mating, the male tiger leaves and the female is left on her own to give birth and raise her cubs.

A female tiger is **pregnant** for four months. She gives birth to between one and four cubs. Tiger cubs are born blind and are about the size of a house cat. They open their eyes after 10 to 14 days. The cubs feed on their mother's milk for the first six months.

The female tiger produces plenty of milk for her cubs. Milk contains all the nutrients that tiger cubs need to grow.

Cub teeth

Cubs are born with milk teeth. Their adult teeth start to grow at about six months. The milk teeth are not pushed out in the same way as human milk teeth. Instead, the adult teeth grow beside the milk teeth and only when the cubs are well-grown do their milk teeth fall out. This means that young tigers never have gaps in their teeth, which might stop them from feeding properly.

Tiger

Often, one of the cubs dies shortly after birth. This is usually the smallest cub, called the runt.

fact

When the cubs have fed, the mother licks them clean.

Growing up

For the first eight weeks, tiger cubs stay in the den where they were born. This is a dangerous time. If they are found by **predators**, such as jackals or pythons, they will be killed. When the cubs are older, they follow their mother into the forest. Tiger cubs are dependent on their mother for the first eighteen months of their life.

Adult female tigers produce a litter of cubs every two years.

Tiger

Sadly, only about half of all tiger cubs survive to two years of age.

fact

One of the cubs will be bolder than the others and will always get to the food first.

Growing and learning

Young males grow faster than the female cubs. By the time they are a year old, the male cubs are much larger. As they get older, the cubs become braver and may spend a whole day alone. By the time they are about two years old, the cubs are ready to live on their own.

Play-fighting is important as it helps young cubs learn to hunt.

Tiger movement

All cats walk on their toes. Tigers can move extremely fast over short distances, but they can't keep this speed up for very long.

When a tiger runs, only a single paw touches the ground at any one time.

14

Jumping and swimming

Tigers can jump. The back legs of the tiger are longer than its front legs. This means they can jump large distances of up to 23 feet. Tigers are also powerful swimmers. In South-East Asia, tigers spend a lot of their time in rivers or swamps, hunting fish and turtles.

Tigers are known to have made vertical leaps of up to 6½ feet.

Tiger facts

- **Tigers have thirty vertebrae in their backbone—that's five more than humans.**
- **The skeletons of the lion and tiger are so alike that, without the skin, it is almost impossible to tell them apart.**

Teaching cubs

Tigers have to teach their cubs to swim. The mother goes into the water and calls to her cubs to follow. If this doesn't work, she will grab the cubs and drop them into the water!

Carnivores

Tigers are carnivores, which means that they eat other animals. They prey on large, hoofed mammals, such as deer and wild pigs. Tigers have strong, hooked claws. The hook shape allows the tiger to grip its **prey** and pull it to the ground.

Tigers' claws can be 5 inches long.

An adult tiger has thirty teeth.

Tiger teeth

As tigers get older, their teeth grow larger. They have small incisor teeth at the front of the mouth, to grip prey and pull meat. Behind the incisors are four long, sharp teeth called canines. Canines are used to stab prey. Behind the canines are large teeth called molars. These are for eating meat and bone. Tigers also have powerful jaws, which allow them to bite easily.

The tiger has huge shoulders, for lifting and dragging its prey.

Tiger

Tiger canine teeth are about 4 inches long, nearly the length of the middle finger of an adult man.

fact

Hunting tigers

Tigers hunt alone and at night. When a tiger finds **prey**, it creeps until it is about 30 feet away, and then rushes forward to knock the prey to the ground. The tiger seizes the prey with its claws, and then drags the body under cover to eat it.

A tiger eats until it is full, and then covers the remains with leaves and soil. It returns when it is hungry to feed some more. A tiger needs to kill once a week, but a female tiger with cubs has to find food every five or six days.

A tiger usually eats about 11 pounds of meat in a night.

Learning to hunt

Cubs watch their mother hunt and kill prey. As they get older, the mother catches prey and allows her cubs to kill it. Eventually they practice hunting on their own, starting with small prey, such as birds, **rodents**, and young deer.

Tiger

Although tigers are skillful hunters, only about one in every ten or twenty attempts is successful.

fact

Tiger senses

Tigers need good eyesight because they hunt at night. Their eyes are positioned at the front of their head and bulge to give them a wide view. Despite their good eyesight, tigers find it hard to see objects that are still. An animal that is only 16 feet away may be invisible to the tiger unless it moves. But a tiger can spot the slightest ear twitch!

Tigers' eyes are large so that they capture as much light as possible in the dark.

Tiger hearing

The tiger's hearing is its best sense. A tiger can tell the difference between leaves rustling in the breeze and the sound of an animal brushing through the undergrowth. Tigers can identify different types of animals from the sounds the animals make when they move.

Tiger fact

A tiger's eyes are often described as being the brightest of any animal.

Sight and hearing are the tiger's most important senses.

Living in a territory

Tigers live alone in an area called a **territory**. Territories differ in size and can be fairly small if there's plenty of **prey**. Both male and female tigers may have their own territory.

Tigers mark the edge of their territory with their scent. They rub their head and chest on trees. These smells warn other tigers to stay away.

If a male tiger enters another male's territory, there is usually a fight. The winner will take over the territory.

Tiger

Tigers usually live in the same territory for life. They only move if food runs out, or if another tiger beats them in a fight.

fact

Finding a territory

A female tiger raises her family in her territory. When her cubs reach about two years of age, they have to establish their own territory. Young females often find a territory close to their mother, but the males move farther away to find a suitable territory.

This tiger is sniffing scent on the ground.

Tiger communication

Tigers can't purr like a house cat. They make sounds such as grunts, moans, growls, and snarls. Tigers growl when they are being **aggressive**. A growl may turn into a hiss or a spit. Tigers swish their tails from side to side and hold their heads low with their eyes open wide and their mouths closed.

A tiger's roar can carry for more than 2 miles through the forest.

Tiger fact

All tigers have a white spot on the back of their ears. Tigers twist their ears around to show this spot as a warning to other tigers.

This tiger is defending itself; its ears are back and it is showing its teeth.

Tiger defenses

Tigers act differently if they are being **defensive**. They snarl, flatten their ears against their heads, and show their teeth. Their eyes become narrow and their tails are held low.

Tiger greetings

A female tiger often moans softly to call her cubs. When tigers of the same family meet, they may make a friendly sneeze or snort, called a "chuff." They then greet each other by rubbing faces.

Tiger cubs soon learn that some of the sounds their mother makes are warnings and other sounds are friendly.

Getting older

Tigers have a difficult life. Many tigers die young because of injury or lack of food. Male tigers may be killed in a fight.

Usually, only one or two cubs from a female's litter survive to adulthood.

This is an old tiger called Charger. He has been in TV documentaries and featured in books.

Life span

Most tigers die before they reach ten years old. Often older tigers starve to death because their teeth are damaged or fall out, so they can't kill **prey**. Tigers live to about twenty years old in a zoo.

Tiger

The oldest known tiger lived to twenty-six years in a zoo.

fact

Tigers in zoos are well fed and live much longer than wild tigers.

Tigers under threat

Just 100 years ago there were 100,000 tigers roaming the Earth. Now there are no more than 7,000.

Tigers have lost their **habitats** because forests have been cut down by humans. Tigers need large areas of forest to find enough food, and to breed.

Hunted by humans

Many tigers are killed by humans. They are hunted for their fur or their bones.

National parks attract a lot of tourists who want to see the tigers.

Saving the tigers

Tigers can be saved if their habitat is protected and hunting is stopped. In India and Nepal, some of the tiger forests have been made into national parks. This means the forests will never be cut down. Some of the rarer tigers are kept in zoos for breeding. Hopefully, in the future, the tigers will be released back into the wild.

Tiger skins and other body parts are sold illegally for large amounts of money.

29

Life cycle

Tiger cubs stay with their mother for two years. Then they leave her to live alone. They find their own territory. In the wild, tigers may live to about 10 years of age.

Two-month-old cubs

Eight-ten-month-old cubs

A four-year-old tiger

A twenty-year-old tiger

Glossary

aggressive being hostile, attacking something or someone

defensive defending something, being protective

endangered animals that may become extinct if something is not done to protect them

extinct no longer in existence

habitat the place where an animal or plant lives

mammal an animal that is covered in hair and gives birth to live young, rather than laying eggs. Female mammals produce milk to feed their young

predator an animal that hunts other animals

pregnant a female animal that has a baby, or babies, developing inside her

prey an animal that is hunted by other animals

rodent an animal, such as a rat or mouse, with large front teeth for gnawing food and wood

territory an area where a tiger spends its life, and where it finds all its food

Index